ORGANIZATIONAL ARRANGEMENTS
TO FACILITATE GLOBAL
MANAGEMENT OF FISHERIES

ORGANIZATIONAL ARRANGEMENTS TO FACILITATE GLOBAL MANAGEMENT OF FISHERIES

Edward Miles

Paper no. 4 in a series prepared for
THE PROGRAM OF INTERNATIONAL STUDIES OF
FISHERY ARRANGEMENTS
Francis T. Christy, Jr., Director

RESOURCES FOR THE FUTURE, INC.
Washington, D.C.

June 1974

Resources for the Future is a nonprofit corporation for research and
education in the development, conservation, and use of natural resources
and the improvement of the quality of the environment. It was established
in 1952 with the cooperation of the Ford Foundation. Part of the work of
Resources for the Future is carried out by its resident staff; part is supported by grants to universities and other nonprofit organizations. Unless
otherwise stated, interpretations and conclusions in RFF publications are
those of the authors; the organization takes responsibility for the selection
of significant subjects for study, the competence of the researchers, and
their freedom of inquiry. The manuscript was edited by Judy Conmy and
Joan Tron.

RFF editors: Mark Reinsberg, Joan R. Tron, Ruth B. Haas, Margaret
Ingram

RFF—PISFA Paper 4. $1.00

Contents

Preface

THE THIRD UNITED NATIONS CONFERENCE ON THE LAW OF THE SEA
opened at the end of 1973 and will begin its first substantive
sessions in June 1974. Of the many problems that will face the
conference delegates, those dealing with the management and
distribution of marine fisheries are among the most important,
most difficult, and least understood. Almost all coastal states
have an interest in marine fisheries. Even though this interest may
be rudimentary, there is still a political constituency that will have
an influence on the decisions of the delegations. The problems of
fisheries are difficult because many stocks of fish have migratory
patterns that extend beyond the jurisdictions of single states, either
paralleling the coast into the waters of neighboring states or
outwards into the high seas. And with present trends towards the
dissolution of the principle of the "freedom of the seas" for
fishing, joint decisions on the distribution of the seas' wealth
become necessary. In the past, fishery decisions have generally
been made on specific problems by fishery experts. With the
coming conference, however, the decisions will be made in a
global arena, in the broad context of a multitude of ocean issues,
and by delegates with only a partial knowledge of fishery matters.

For these reasons Resources for the Future decided to con-
centrate its current ocean interests on fisheries and, with the
help of a supplemental grant from the Ford Foundation, initiated
the Program of International Studies of Fishery Arrangements.
The objective of the program is to produce information that will
facilitate the preparations for the UN Conference and contribute
to the process of making decisions. The program approaches this
objective by concentrating primarily on particular fisheries and
fishery regions, attempting to elucidate the variety of alternatives
that exist in different, real situations. It is hoped that this will
produce a better understanding of the implications of the proposals for universal regimes and principles that are likely to emerge
in the UN discussions. In addition, the program examines some
of the generic problems of fisheries management, distribution, and
institutions.

Each study provides background information on recent developments and trends and a discussion of alternative legal and institutional arrangements for the resolution of the problems. The studies attempt to raise questions and suggest approaches that will be helpful to the decision makers, rather than to recommend specific courses of action. Every effort has been made to ensure that each study has been prepared from a non-national perspective and that it has taken into account all responsible points of view and interests. The studies are freely available to all delegates at the UN Conference. In addition, the program seeks opportunities for full and free discussion of the studies with interested persons. Eventually all of the separate studies may be put together in a single volume in order to meet the anticipated continuing demand for information on fishery arrangements. Comments and criticisms of the individual papers are solicited and will be considered for publication in such a volume.

Studies in the program include:

An overview of fishery arrangements;
North Pacific fisheries management;
East Central Atlantic fisheries;
Indian Ocean fisheries;
Southeast Asia fisheries;
World tuna fisheries;
Alternative international institutions;
Future fishery problems.

The present study deals with the prospects for a global fisheries agency. It discusses the trends that are taking place in fisheries and the effects that these are likely to have on the functions that a global agency, such as the FAO, might fulfill. It is not expected that the functions of the FAO will change significantly; that is, the FAO will continue to have little more than an advisory role in the formulation and adoption of regulations, enforcement of regulations, and the resolution of conflicts. However, the critical role of the FAO in the provision of information for fisheries management will become far more important than it has been in the past. The demand for information, deriving from the changes taking place in fisheries and in the law of the sea, will require greatly increased support of a global fisheries agency.

Dr. Edward Miles is Professor of Marine Studies and Public Affairs at the University of Washington and was formerly Associate Professor of International Relations at the School of

International Studies, University of Denver. He specializes in studies of international organization and, in addition to his work in ocean management, has done considerable research on international organization for space exploration.

FRANCIS T. CHRISTY, JR., Director
RFF Program of International
Studies of Fishery Arrangements

Introduction

THE PRIMARY TASK of this paper is to identify and evaluate the range of functional possibilities available for a global fisheries agency. Traditionally, the functions required by the process of international fisheries management have been the collection, analysis, and dissemination of data; the framing and implementation of conservation regulations, including the assessment of the effects of these regulations on the yields of fisheries; the resolution of conflict between the parties involved in any fishery; and the enforcement of regulatory decisions. The analysis undertaken here will attempt to determine whether and in what ways current trends in technology and jurisdictional claims on the part of coastal states have changed or will change the ways in which these functions are performed at the global level.

These four functions—research, regulation, conflict resolution, and enforcement—have significantly different requirements with regard to the exercise of authority. It must also be recognized that there are important differences in the conditions under which fishery activities are carried out and that these affect the distribution of authority

There are basically three types of situations governing the exercise of authority in fisheries: (1) those involving stocks which are under the complete control of a single coastal state; (2) those involving stocks which, as a result of their range of migration, give rise to the sharing of jurisdiction between two or more coastal states; and (3) those involving highly migratory oceanic species, freely moving between the jurisdictions of coastal states and the high seas or even entirely outside national jurisdictions.

It is assumed that extensions of exclusive coastal-state jurisdiction up to 200 miles will affect the first type of situation to the extent that more stocks will fall under the complete control of coastal states than is currently the case. In this situation there is

NOTE: The research for this paper has been supported by Resources for the Future, as one of several monographs in its Program of International Studies of Fishery Arrangements. The sponsor should in no way be held responsible for the views expressed herein. The author wishes to thank the following people for reacting critically to an earlier draft of the manuscript: F. W. G. Baker, William Burke, Francis Christy, Jr., Vincent Davis, Ernst Haas, Joseph Nye, Jr., Giulio Pontecorvo, and Lawrence Veit. Special thanks are due to Francis Christy for outstanding editorial contributions.

very little that a global fisheries organization could do, although, as we shall see, there are limited possibilities. The second sort of situation, however, is important, because of the necessity for joint decisions among states sharing the resource. There are more possibilities for a global agency here and perhaps under the third type of situation. These possibilities will be outlined in subsequent sections of the paper.

The first part of this exercise will be a brief summary of the salient political characteristics of current attempts to manage world fisheries. As with many questions of public policy, recommendations on organizational arrangements have to be evaluated with respect both to their desirability and to the likelihood of their acceptance and implementation. What is desirable and what is workable do not often coincide, and the case of fisheries management is no exception. Thus, a basic assumption in this paper is that feasibility always depends on the political process in which the proposed mechanism is to operate, hence the initial concern with describing that process. The second part of the analysis will be an examination of the effects of new trends and developments on the probable functions of a global agency. The third and final part will consist of suggestions on how such an agency might accommodate its new or enlarged functions.

I Political Process of International Fisheries Management

THE REGULATORY IMPLICATIONS of fisheries as a common property resource are well known and have been analyzed in detail by many specialists. The basic conditions are that "no single user has exclusive use rights to the resource nor can he prevent others from sharing in its exploitation."[1] Since the states using the same shared resource may have different interests in the resource, it is extremely difficult to arrive at a system of unified management which achieves an effective balance among the four goals enunciated by Christy in this series. These are: the optimization of biological yields, the optimization of social and economic yields, the reduction of management costs, and the achievement of acceptable patterns of the distribution of wealth.[2]

Not only are the objectives multiple, but, as pursued by different states, they may also be incompatible. For instance, the maximization of economic yields through control of the amount of effort applied in exploiting a fishery usually reduces the level of employment in a country's fisheries industry. Where conflicting objectives are not readily resolvable, management tends to become ineffective, and this often leads to the depletion of both resources and profitability of fishing industries. The problem is accentuated by growth in demand for fish and technological advances because higher prices and lower costs make it economically possible for more fishermen to be satisfied with the lower levels of catch of depleted stocks. Furthermore, management practices which are aimed solely at maintaining the maximum

---

[1] Francis T. Christy, Jr., and Anthony Scott, *The Common Wealth in Ocean Fisheries* (Baltimore: The Johns Hopkins Press for Resources for the Future, Inc., 1965), p. 6.
[2] Francis T. Christy, Jr., *Alternative Arrangements for Marine Fisheries: An Overview*, Resources for the Future Program of International Studies of Fishery Arrangements, Paper no. 1 (Washington, D.C., 1973), Ch. 2. See also Ralph Turvey, "Optimization and Suboptimization in Fishery Regulation," *American Economic Review,* vol. 54 (March 1964), pp. 64–76; Giulio Pontecorvo, "Optimization and Taxation in an Open-Access Resource: The Fishery," in Mason Gaffney, ed., *Extractive Resources and Taxation* (Madison: University of Wisconsin Press, 1967), pp. 157–167; B. J. Rothschild, "Questions of Strategy in Fishery Management and Development," and D. L. Alverson, "Objectives and Problems of Management of Living Resources of the Ocean" (Papers presented at the FAO Technical Conference on Fishery Management and Development, Vancouver, February 13–23, 1973).

1

physical yield of the stock, e.g., a limit on the total catch, often lead to increasing the number of vessels applied, thereby increasing the resultant waste.[3]

On the other hand, effective management controls generally have a direct effect on the distribution of income from fisheries, and therefore raise intractable political problems. These inherent difficulties are made even greater by the fact that a large number of countries, sometimes with widely differing wage/price structures and conflicting national goals, must attempt to make regulatory decisions through bargaining with each other, emphasizing the search for acceptable compromises rather than some optimum balance among the goals of management.

One consequence of the inability to achieve unified management of the resource is that the benefits become highly divisible, so that, from the perspective of each individual negotiator, the gains of others are losses he must bear. This is a very familiar problem in international relations, and it is characterized by a lack of trust among the participants. This mutual distrust maximizes the incentive for each participant to insist on retaining a veto regarding the implementation of any agreements that are arrived at.[4] According to Singer:

> When there is little trust between the players, there is a strong temptation for each to assume that the other will think only of his own interests, but in pursuing their separate strategies of *individual* rationality, their joint behavior is one of collective irrationality.[5]

Not only does the structure of the political process lead to ineffective decisions when large numbers of players pursue conflicting goals but, more importantly, there is a self-reinforcing quality about it, because each participant attempts to retain the widest discretion over whatever decisions are taken.

[3] This summary is based on Christy and Scott, *Common Wealth,* pp. 7, 9–10, and 14–16. See also Francis T. Christy, Jr., "Fisheries Goals and Rights of Property," *Transactions of the American Fisheries Society,* vol. 98, no. 2 (April 1969), pp. 309–378; and James A. Crutchfield, "Overcapitalization of Fishing Effort," in Lewis M. Alexander, ed., *The Future of the Sea's Resources* (Kingston: University of Rhode Island, Law of the Sea Institute, 1968), pp. 23–27. 23–27.

[4] Robert L. Bish, "An Economic Approach to Land and Water Resource Management: A Report on the Puget Sound Study" (Paper presented to the Western Agricultural Economic Research Council, San Francisco, October 25–26, 1971), pp. 8, 17.

[5] J. David Singer, *The Scientific Study of Politics: An Approach to Foreign Policy Analysis* (New York: General Learning Press, 1972), p. 20.

2

PRESENT FISHERIES ARRANGEMENTS

It is not surprising that the conditions and problems described above have resulted in highly restricted terms of reference for most regulatory fishery commissions. The present arrangements for fishery management are defined in terms of specific portions of the world ocean and/or species. Using the criterion of type of task to differentiate among existing organizations, the FAO identifies three sorts of regional commissions: those dealing mainly with research, even though they may offer advice and recommendations on conservation measures; regulatory commissions in which the supporting research is done within member countries; and regulatory commissions in which the supporting research is done by their own staffs.[6]

There are deficiencies both with respect to the amount of authority delegated to the organization and to the scope of its domain. For instance, since compliance is voluntary and universality in the acceptance of decisions is a necessary condition for effectiveness, most regional commissions can only make recommendations. Others may make recommendations that are potentially binding, if there are no objections within a stipulated period of time, while only a very few may issue binding decisions.

CONCLUSIONS

Recommendations on future organizational arrangements at the global level must always take into account the fact that the structure of the political process of international fisheries management, as currently practiced, inherently greatly restricts regional

[6] See the excellent \paper prepared by the Food and Agriculture Organization, Department of Fisheries, *International Fishery Bodies* (Doc. no. COFI/66/6), 20 May 1966, pp. 8–9. See also William Burke, "Aspects of Decision-Making Processes in Intergovernmental Fishery Commissions," *Washington Law Review,* vol. 43, no. 115 (1967), pp. 115–178; J. E. Carroz, "La commission internationale des pêches pour l'Atlantique Sud-Est," *Annuaire canadien de droit international 1971,* pp. 3–29; J. E. Carroz and A. G. Roche, "The Proposed International Commission for the Conservation of Atlantic Tunas," *American Journal of International Law,* vol. 61 (1967), pp. 673–702; Wilbert M. Chapman, "The Theory and Practice of International Fishery Development Management," *San Diego Law Review,* vol. 7, no. 3 (July 1970), pp. 408–454; Christy and Scott, *Common Wealth,* pp. 204–297; John L. Kask, "Present Arrangements for Fishery Exploitation," in Alexander, ed., *Sea's Resources,* pp. 56–61; and C. E. Lucas, *International Fishery Bodies of the North Atlantic,* Law of the Sea Institute, Occasional Paper no. 5 (Kingston: University of Rhode Island, 1970).

as well as global organizations. Moreover, the current trends in the preparatory negotiations on the Law of the Sea and in the actions of a considerable number of coastal states lead toward an extension of coastal-state authority over living resources of the ocean. For these reasons, we cannot expect major expansions in the authority of global organizations in the near future. The limits of feasibility lie here.

As Olson points out, it is not only necessary to ask whether a formal organization exists or whether even informal cooperation exists in a given situation. What is most important is "whether there is a sufficient degree of organized or cooperative effort" for the system to provide the optimal amount of control.[7] In international fisheries management, this clearly does not exist.[8]

Olson argues further:

> We already have many international organizations—perhaps about as many as we would want—yet national governments are unwilling to give up what they would have to give up to allow these international organizations to deal adequately with the international problems allocated to them. Thus we should ask under what conditions independent countries will do what is needed to carry informal cooperation of formal organization to a more nearly optimal point.[9]

[7] Mancur Olson, "Increasing the Incentives for International Cooperation," *International Organization,* vol. 25, no. 4 (Autumn 1971), p. 867.

[8] Wilbert M. Chapman, "Fishery Resources in Offshore Waters," in Lewis M. Alexander, ed., *The Law of the Sea* (Columbus: Ohio State University Press, 1967), pp. 98, 102.

[9] Olson, "International Cooperation," p. 867.

II Recent Trends and New Demands in Managing World Fisheries

THE NEW DEVELOPMENTS and trends in fisheries include the considerable increase in effort and the mobility of the new vessels, the decline of the rate of increase in total world catch, and increasing conflicts between local and nonlocal fishing states, giving impetus to the movement to extend exclusive jurisdiction over fisheries by the coastal state.[10] These trends have already been analyzed in some detail by others, but, for present purposes, the management implications are most important, because they may create new functional demands or modify old ones for regional and global fisheries organizations.

The demands for management generated as a consequence of these trends have been described in a series of papers by the FAO Department of Fisheries. Perhaps the most significant development in world fisheries management is the fact that technological advance, particularly increased mobility of vessels, has created a real need for global coordination of management measures decided upon in different regions. This is because restrictions applied to levels of efforts or length of seasons in one region very quickly have impacts on other regions, since fleets can easily be diverted to profitable fishing grounds elsewhere in the world. Moreover, conservation regulations will seldom be adequate if taken in isolation from the other fisheries with which particular species interact. As Saila and Norton have noted: "Not only is management therefore a worldwide problem, but fewer opportunities now exist to escape the consequences of failure to achieve rational management of one stock by diversion of the excess capacity to other stocks still underexploited."[11]

Obviously, it is easier to deal with the problem of mobility if

---

[10] For good summaries on this last problem, see John Weddin, "Impact of Distant Water on Coastal Fisheries," in Alexander, ed., *Sea's Resources,* pp. 14–18; John Gulland, J. P. Troadec, and E. O. Bayagbona, "Management and Development of Fisheries in the Eastern Central Atlantic," *Technical Conference on Fishery Management and Development, Vancouver, Canada, 13–23 February 1973,* Doc. FI: D/73/R-7 (Rome: Food and Agriculture Organization, 1973) and John Gulland, "Distant Water Fisheries and their Relation to Development and Management," *Technical Conference,* Doc. FI: D/73/R-11.

[11] Saul Saila and Virgil Norton, "Alternative Arrangements for the Management of Tuna," Resources for the Future Program of International Studies of Fishery Arrangements, Paper no. 6, early draft.

5

the stocks are within the exclusive jurisdiction of a single coastal state, as access can be controlled. The problem becomes much more difficult in the two remaining situations, when jurisdiction over the resource is shared by two or more coastal states, or when the resource is a highly migratory oceanic species. With jurisdiction shared, pressures will increase for coastal states to arrive at agreement on common methods for dealing with management problems in each jurisdiction. This has already emerged in the Gulf of Guinea, and it is a distinct possibility for both the east and west coasts of South America. With respect to highly migratory species, there will have to be coordination of management measures between local and nonlocal fishing countries and also among nonlocals themselves, if large portions of the catch are taken in waters outside of any national jurisdiction and in different oceans.[12]

Increased mobility of fishing vessels has another effect on regional commissions; it requires that such agencies be able to act quickly.[13] This means that it may be necessary for regulations to be imposed before a stock has been depleted and perhaps on the basis of incomplete scientific information. But the system of international fisheries management as described here is a very decentralized one. The decision-making process is very slow, since every participant has a veto. Moreover, conservation regulations cannot work unless all players follow the rules. If they do not, he who cheats wins.

IMPLICATIONS

What are the implications of such developments for management of world fisheries? The response of many coastal states has been to extend their exclusive jurisdiction over fishing to 200 miles, or to the outer edge of the continental shelf, or to some combination of depth and distance.[14]

Some effects of this are likely to be immediate, notably the

---

[12] Food and Agriculture Organization, Department of Fisheries, *Conservation Problems with Special Reference to the New Technology* (FAO Fisheries Circular no. 139), 1972, p. 9. See also Food and Agriculture Organization, Committee on Fisheries, *Emergent Fishery Problems of an International Character* (Doc. no. COFI/66/8), 16 May 1969, p. 2.

[13] Food and Agriculture Organization, Department of Fisheries, *Conservation Problems*, pp. 5, 9.

[14] These developments have already been analyzed in some detail. The reader is referred to Hiroshi Kasahara, "Extension of Fishery Jurisdiction," in Lewis M.

exclusion of some foreign fishing fleets from certain coastal waters; others are essentially long-term, e.g., attempts by these foreign fishing fleets to accommodate the demands of developing coastal states for establishing joint venture arrangements, the extraction of economic rent, and the like.

With respect to immediate effects, the general trend will be against all foreign distant-water fleets, but some will be harder hit than others. At first, the highly mobile fleets will attempt to shift location, but if these extensions of jurisdiction are generalized throughout the world ocean, there will be few real opportunities to do so. The less mobile fleets (e.g., the UK trawler fleets off Iceland) will have to seek some immediate accommodation. Temporary hardships might also be experienced where a foreign fishing fleet has been excluded from a particular stock it has fished for a long time. In fact, this type of situation might lead to increases in domestic unemployment for countries like the United Kingdom; such unemployment decreases government flexibility in trying to come to terms with coastal states which have extended their jurisdiction. As one economist put it: "You may adjust in the capital market but adjustment in the labor market will be a much harder political problem for countries like the UK, France and Norway."[15]

This problem raises the question of whether participation in a fishery by foreign fleets will be obligatory or merely permissible in the new conventions on the Law of the Sea currently being negotiated. If, as some proposals would have it, the convention declares that coastal states *shall* permit foreign fishing for resources it cannot fully utilize, then the problem for the nonlocals will be considerably eased. If, however, the convention declares that the coastal states *may* permit such fishing, then the difficulty previously described will arise, since some states undoubtedly will wish to exclude all foreign fishing fleets. This could lead to a decline in total world catch if generally applied,

---

Alexander, ed., *The Law of the Sea: A New Geneva Conference* (Kingston: University of Rhode Island, Law of the Sea Institute, 1972), pp. 101–103; John A. Knauss, *Factors Influencing a U. S. Position in a Future Law of the Sea Conference*, Sea Grant Publication no. WIS-SG–72–112 (Madison: University of Wisconsin, 1972), pp. 190–199; Francis T. Christy, Jr., "Implications for Fisheries of the U. S. Draft Convention on the Sea Bed" (Paper presented to the Marine Technology Symposium on the Law of the Sea: A Year of Crisis, 1972); and Francis T. Christy, Jr., "Fisheries Problems and the U. S. Draft Article," *Proceedings of Fourth National Sea Grant Conference*, pp. 200–217.

[15] Private communication from Giulio Pontecorvo, Professor of Economics, Columbia University School of Business.

but this is unlikely, since other states may wish to trade fishing rights for other benefits unrelated to the fishery.

Correspondingly, where developing coastal states possessing significant resources make demands for capital investment in their fisheries as the price of participation by foreign fleets, the incentives for nonlocals to engage in joint ventures will increase. The underlying motivation here will be the utilization of joint ventures either as a means of ensuring continued fishing or for securing orderly disinvestment.[16]

It is at least conceivable in this situation that the utilities of management for both local and nonlocal fishing countries may become somewhat more symmetrically related. Adequate conservation of the resource will be an interest flowing both from the desire to protect investments and from the perceived importance of fisheries as a foreign exchange earner. Thus, it may be easier to arrive at agreement between local and nonlocal fishing countries than between a number of neighboring coastal states. More specifically, such arrangements will increase problems of allocation between coastal states sharing particular stocks. Some examples of this can already be seen in certain parts of the world, e.g., between Brazil and Argentina, Peru and Chile, in Southeast Asia generally, and in the Mediterranean Sea between Morocco and Spain. The fact is that, while most nonlocals can afford to pay much for participation in a fishery, neighbors are sometimes not in a position to do so, and this adds to the difficulty.

It should be emphasized, however, that joint ventures which require both parties to make significant investments in a fishery are not the only alternative open to developing countries. Licensing agreements also would allow the production of revenues without the requirement that these revenues be reinvested in the fishery. It is very likely that, in the future, nonlocal fishing countries will wish to seek regional coordination in the setting of license fees, rather than have each coastal state do so separately, in order to provide the required stability for their investment. Obviously, many developing countries will not at first find this procedure attractive, but the nonlocal countries may be in a strong position. Because many developing coastal states cannot utilize high-priced resources on a vast scale, they would not be able to derive significant income from them if nonlocal fishing countries refused to exploit a particular resource because of

---

[16] I am indebted for this point to James Crutchfield, Professor of Economics, University of Washington.

8

excessive taxes, fees, or restrictions. They will generally find it more to their advantage to collect economic or other benefits from foreign fishermen than to prohibit foreign fishing entirely.

FUNCTIONAL REQUISITES
OF A GLOBAL ORGANIZATION

Given the trends and implications described above, what functions will a global agency be required to perform? It would appear that the functions are generally of three types—coordination, research, and education and training.

As stated earlier, fleet mobility has made fisheries management at the regional and local level inadequate. There is a growing need for some global unit to concern itself with the coordination of conservation measures decided upon in different regional commissions. This is particularly true in the Atlantic and Pacific oceans, where many species are now heavily exploited. But the task will be a difficult and complex one, since in some parts of the world regional commissions will decline in significance as a result of extensions in exclusive coastal-state jurisdiction. The management problem, however, with respect to species which migrate through jurisdictions or of highly migratory species will remain. Thus, the need for evaluating the consequences of regulations adopted in different parts of the world will continue to exist.

A global organization like the FAO has the opportunity to perform several functions in facilitating arrangements between coastal and foreign states. The first step lies in providing information and other services to developing countries on the process of entering into joint ventures. This should ensure that both parties fully understand the nature of their reciprocal rights and duties, that everything is actually provided for in the agreement, and that developing countries in particular have adequate information on what the alternatives are.

Another function relates to the education of appropriate authorities in each developing country on their responsibilities concerning the multiple objectives of management. On the basis of agreements currently being discussed in the Indian Ocean area, for instance, joint ventures may be adopted without regard to the necessity for conservation. There may be a greater awareness of the need for conservation measures in conjunction with joint ventures in the countries bordering the Gulf of Guinea. But clearly a major continuing task of both the Indian Ocean Fishery

Commission (IOFC) and the Commission for East Central Atlantic Fisheries (CECAF) revolves around this kind of question, and, to be sure, CECAF has already begun to make encouraging moves in this direction.

The research function which could be performed by a global agency includes work on stock assessment and evaluating the probable consequences of alternative management measures adopted in different regions of the world. Another such function relates to the economic analysis underlying the setting of license fees. For instance, there are signs (particularly from France vis-à-vis countries bordering the Gulf of Guinea) that foreign fishing fleets may prefer to seek regional coordination in the setting of license fees and in the imposition of controls on fishing as a mechanism for avoiding the capriciousness of any single state. But there are reasons why such regional coordination may also be in the interest of developing coastal states in situations where the stocks are shared by several states. The nonlocal fishermen will obviously want to fish where the costs are lowest. Unless fees are coordinated, there could be a competitive relationship between neighboring states that would be mutually destructive. That is, if one state lowered its fees in order to attract more nonlocal fishermen, there would be a temptation for other states to respond, with the result that the fees would become too low to achieve management objectives, and none of the local states would be receiving appropriate revenues or benefits.

The coordination of fees, for the purposes of both stability and the maintenance of satisfactory benefits for local states, may require significantly expanded responsibilities for the various regional commissions. In particular, it may be necessary to engage in economic analyses of the values of fishing rights in order to provide a basis for negotiating these rights and coordinating the fees. But developing coastal states do not possess much of this kind of expertise, and regional commissions may find the acquisition of such talent difficult. There may well be significant economies of scale in having a global organization maintain a pool of competent analysts to provide this service.

METHOD OF BARGAINING

It is assumed that extensions of coastal-state jurisdiction will in the short run put great emphasis on bilateral or multilateral bargaining on such issues as access and the amount of rent to be extracted. But it should be noted that the perspective from which the bargaining is approached is important. For instance, within regional regulatory commissions, the traditional method of negotiating agreements restricts the negotiator's focus to calculating immediate costs and benefits along a single substantive dimension—that of shares in the resource. This eliminates the possibility of constructing viable package deals which serve to broaden the definition of benefits available to all participants. [17]

If package deals were to be created, access to a fishery or increased shares of a particular stock could be traded off, for instance, for investment in agricultural projects, or certain kinds of education and training, or textiles. It is instructive in this regard to look at the experience of the European Economic Community in resolving thorny problems of agricultural policy. Solutions were forthcoming only when members began to define benefits in a framework wider than that of agriculture.[18] When the issues are mixed in this way, it may be possible to increase the incentives for effective compromise.

There are two important caveats to be attached to this recommendation. First, it should be recognized that attempts to trade fishing rights for other values may cause short-run problems for fisheries negotiators and that these may sometimes be severe. As mentioned previously, significant restrictions on access to fishing grounds where much activity has historically been concentrated may cause dislocations in domestic labor markets, and these will have political effects. The point is that such dislocations are likely to occur anyway, but their impacts may be lessened selectively through adopting more flexible definitions of gains and losses in the bargaining. Secondly, the assumption that mutually profitable trade-offs within the field of fisheries negotiation can be arranged by broadening the definition of benefits holds only if one begins with a substantive interest in optimizing the goals of management. If one begins from another end, e.g., optimizing security interests, broadening the definition of benefits to be traded off may not be compatible with optimizing the goals of fisheries management: at that point, fisheries interests become part of a much wider negotiation in which the basic tradeoff is between all marine resources, on the one hand, and navigational rights on the other.

---

[17] Private communication from Ernst Haas, Professor of Political Science, Institute of International Studies, University of California (Berkeley).

[18] See Leon Lindberg and Stuart Scheingold, *Europe's Would-Be Polity* (Englewood Cliffs, N.J.: Prentice-Hall, Inc., 1971), p. 158.

III Organizational Arrangements and Functional Possibilities

ASSUMPTIONS

SEVERAL ASSUMPTIONS underlie the arrangements to be described here. The first is that, given the political process of international fisheries management analyzed in an earlier section of this paper, we cannot expect major increases in the authority of global organizations. More specifically, with respect to resources shared by two or more coastal states, we cannot expect a global research agency to operate in strikingly different fashion from the way the FAO (i.e., Department of Fisheries and Committee on Fisheries) has operated, particularly since 1964. Finally, the possibilities outlined need not be decided upon at the current Law of the Sea negotiations. This last assumption requires some explanation.

From the fisheries perspective, the primary focus at the Law of the Sea negotiations will be on jurisdiction. Only a very few proposals include assumptions about management policies, e.g., the U.S. and Canadian proposals distinguishing management requirements for anadromous and highly migratory species. The recommendations offered in this paper speak more to the translation of jurisdiction into policy once the extent of coastal-states rights has been decided upon. The organizational arrangements to be discussed here can evolve out of the implementation of policy after the LOS negotiations, and therefore need not be added to the already onerous list of issues to be decided there.

Since current trends toward the extension of coastal-state authority are not supportive of significant increases in the authority of global organizations, there is not much chance of a global fisheries organization operating in a strikingly different fashion from the FAO. There *are* several proposals before the LOS Conference, and outside, which call for the creation of a World Ocean Organization, under which the management of fisheries would be subsumed. It does not appear that this will be a likely outcome of the negotiations, but even if it is, it will not effectively increase authority at the global level or yield the resources necessary to exercise it.

While the clear trend is toward increasing coastal-state author- ity, it has already been argued that the emergence of a 200-mile economic zone is likely to make the management interests of coastal states and nonlocal fishing states more symmetrical. Moreover, since no coastal state will be able by itself to deal adequately with all management problems, a need for some organization to provide global overview and coordination will become apparent. Finally, developing countries will be in even greater need of special expertise and thus of expanded programs in technical assistance, training, and education. Some of this can be derived from joint ventures, but there will be an additional need for a global organization to manage such a program. The FAO has in fact been doing this for many years, and the primary concern in this section of the paper is to spell out how its role can be expanded and its effectiveness increased.

Particular attention will be paid to the experience of the Committee on Fisheries (COFI), as it is an almost complete mirror of world fishery politics, having a membership of seventy-eight countries represented by their senior fishery officers. The Soviet Union and the Chinese People's Republic are not members of the FAO, although Soviet delegates attend COFI meetings as observers and can participate as actively as they wish in the debates.[19] The cross section of views visible within COFI, therefore, relative to the role of a global organization in world fisheries management is not likely to be substantially different in any other forum.

An objection might be raised that COFI will not mirror world *ocean* politics at the LOS Conference, where fisheries will be only one item in the trade-offs. This is correct but irrelevant to the aims here, since recommendations in this paper concern the implementation of policy after the jurisdictional arrangements have been decided upon. In this context COFI will continue to be a mirror of world fishery politics. Finally, the analysis will include a separate account of the possibilities for global regulations concerning highly migratory oceanic species, since the developmental trends here appear demonstrably different from those involving other species. In this connection some special concern will be given to the cases of tuna and whales.

POSSIBILITIES FOR EXPANDING FAO FUNCTIONS

It might be initially assumed that there are currently clear lines of demarcation between COFI as the intergovernmental "execu-

---

[19] On his return from China the Director-General of FAO announced that China would soon rejoin the FAO. *International Herald Tribune,* 13 March 1973.

tive'' unit in world fishery politics and the Department of Fisheries (FID) of FAO as the operating mechanism, implementing decisions arrived at in COFI. This would be incorrect. The lines between COFI and FID are indeed quite blurred—a fact which causes some governmental representatives a certain amount of frustration. One of COFI's tasks is to advise FID on its program, and this it does. But it also performs a latent function by acting as a support to the Assistant Director-General for Fisheries in the FAO Council in budgetary fights with other major sectors of FAO dealing with agriculture and forestry. This blurring of lines allows the Secretariat to exercise significant initiative in determining COFI's agenda and even in influencing the outcome of some discussions. The failure to make a clear distinction between COFI and FAO in the recommendations to follow is therefore not an inadvertant omission in this paper but a deliberate reflection of the ambiguity that many observers recognize.

Ever since the creation of COFI was formally approved by the FAO Conference in 1965, there has been a continuing debate on whether this body should be a creature of the FAO Council (under Article V of the Constitution) or whether it should be transformed into a largely autonomous unit having the capacity to make its own appropriations (under Article XIV). This debate is an important one for the purposes here because it reflects divergent perceptions of FAO's role in global fisheries management activities. There are those who want FAO to stick to its traditional role and eschew any involvement in regulatory responsibilities. Others wish it to play a more independent role in management, but the content of this is never clearly defined. The ambiguity is compounded by the uncertainties surrounding extensions of coastal-states jurisdiction as a result of upcoming Law of the Sea negotiations.

In this context, it is significant that at the Sixth Session in 1971 members appeared to be in agreement on two operational dimensions of COFI's tasks. The first of these was that COFI's primary activity consisted of elaborating general principles for fishery management. The FAO was considered to have its largest role in stock assessment activity, and this carried with it a responsibility in technical assistance for developing countries which lacked the requisite expertise. The second was that FAO (and COFI) had no role in the implementation of management measures. This was purely a regional activity involving treaty-based commissions. "Implementation" includes the issue of enforcement.[20]

On the other hand, there was considerable disagreement on the issue of FAO's role in the formulation of conservation regulations. Those who were opposed to any FAO activity claimed that the diversity of regional conditions made the formulation of general guidelines useless.[21] This position can also be read in part as evidence of the unwillingness of several countries to have a global organization pronouncing upon measures taken in the regions in which they are most interested. This issue is raised in a different form whenever the question of coordination of regional commissions not sponsored by FAO comes up, and one can observe the same kind of division in attitudes. This tension will continue, since several countries would like to see COFI "take a more active part in reviewing regularly the progress of these commissions set up by FAO *and other regional bodies* and consider requesting these bodies to report to the Committee."[22]

This distribution of attitudes is replicated in the replies to the questionnaire distributed by the Department of Fisheries on the functions of COFI to the eighteen members of the Sub-Committee on the Development of Cooperation with International Organizations Concerned with Fisheries. Of eleven replies received by November 20, 1972, seven countries thought that COFI's functions as defined in Rule XXX–6 of the General Rules of the Organization were adequate.[23] These countries were Canada, Japan, Kenya, Nigeria, Norway, Peru, and the United States. Four countries—France, Morocco, Senegal, and Spain—supported expansion of COFI's functions.[24] In its reply the French government made the most far-reaching proposal relative to the need for coordination. It wished to authorize COFI:

> . . . to intervene directly (through resolutions or recommendations, for example) with intergovernmental fisheries protection and devel-

---

[20] Food and Agriculture Organization, Committee on Fisheries, *Report of the Sixth Session of the Committee on Fisheries,* Rome, 15–21 April 1971, p. 8.

[21] *Ibid.,* p. 9.

[22] *Ibid.*

[23] Food and Agriculture Organization, Committee on Fisheries, *Analysis of Replies to Questionnaire on the Functions of the Committee on Fisheries* (Doc. no. COFI/C/3/73/5), December 1972, p. 3.

[24] *Ibid.* For other summaries of this issue, see *ibid.,* Annex 1, p. 6; and Food and Agriculture Organization, Committee on Fisheries, *Inter-governmental Cooperation in the Rational Utilization of Fishery Resources* (Doc. no. COFI/72/6), 7 March 1972.

opment agencies to coordinate and harmonize the actions these agencies have occasion to take. More generally, it appears to us desirable that the Committee on Fisheries serve as a kind of general assembly for the international fisheries commissions with a view to comparison of the solutions adopted and results obtained by each of them so as to enhance the effectiveness of what they do and coordinate it better.[25]

Since the general expectation is that the focus of regulation will remain at the regional level, and since mobility of fishing vessels has created a need for the coordination of regulatory measures taken by different regional fisheries commissions, we should regard the difference of views as to COFI's role in the formulation of conservation measures as an opportunity for growth rather than a problem. Such diversity of views in fact can allow the shaping of alternatives by the leadership. One alternative in pursuing such growth is represented by the French proposal for formal changes in COFI's terms of reference. But what might be the probable costs of choosing this course of action?

In the first place, putting this question on the agenda may well activate a two-dimensional, jurisdictional conflict between the FAO and several regional commissions and between the FAO and several important fishing countries which may act as spokesmen for one or another regional commission. The opposing coalition is likely to be overwhelming. Members of COFI should therefore always be aware that there is a latent conflict of major proportions between developed and developing states within COFI, and care should always be taken to avoid activating a confrontation which could very easily get out of control and seriously impair management efforts. But it is not necessary to make a formal issue of this to achieve the coordination required. COFI's terms of reference are now sufficiently broad to cover this, if it is done carefully. In fact, this is already happening, although perhaps not as quickly as one would like.

For instance, the FAO currently gives assistance to regional commissions in the collection and analysis of data, but it should be noted that there are inadequacies relative to specifying area of capture and level of effort applied by the countries involved, since this information is economically sensitive. Such coordination already exists for the northwest Atlantic, the southwest Atlantic, the east central Atlantic and the Mediterranean. Work has begun

[25] Food and Agriculture Organization, Committee on Fisheries, *Analysis of Replies*, p. 8.

16

on the Indian Ocean.[26] Other examples are the FAO's relationships with the International Commission for the Conservation of Atlantic Tuna (ICCAT) and with the International Whaling Commission (IWC). But it is suggested here that the coordination function be approached in a more comprehensive way. Cooperating in the collection and analysis of data should be considered only the first, easiest, and least controversial level of coordination. There are two additional levels which any global organization will have to consider to varying degrees and which a more active COFI could not escape. The second level refers to the expectation that the organization will inevitably be drawn into the formulation of management principles because it will be the only repository of global information for the widest range of species and because of the increasing need for some unit to provide continuing assessments of the probable impacts—biological, economic, and social—of alternative management measures. Such involvement may not necessarily lead to an increase in conflict between members and to a consequent damage to stock assessment and technical assistance activities. The protection lies in the quality of work done and the relative neutrality of an organization dealing primarily with the collection and analysis of data.

The third level of coordination is the most difficult and controversial, for it deals with such matters as the actual management of species and the setting of limits on size of catch, length of seasons, and level of effort. It is clear that under present circumstances a global organization cannot have a major role here, but it will be effective nevertheless, since there will be a need for coordinating the timing of seasons on particular types of fish, e.g., tuna, between different oceans. The timing of seasons will be especially important, given great fleet mobility, because the choice of dates may have considerable impact on the distribution of income.

With respect to conflict resolution, it is not likely that COFI in the near future will become an independent global actor in resolving disagreements over fisheries. But there is an existing functional demand for such a body to play a fact-finding role, particularly relative to estimating the global consequences of alternative measures which may be adopted. It may be also that

[26] All examples mentioned are taken from Food and Agriculture Organization, Committee on Fisheries, *The Role of the FAO in the Management of Fishery Resources* (Doc. no. COFI/71/8), 30 January 1971. See also Food and Agriculture Organization, Committee on Fisheries, *Some Problems of Management* (Doc. no. COFI/72/4), 11 February 1972, pp. 2–3.

over time coastal states sharing particular stocks, and in conflict over the distribution of income, may wish to involve global research agencies like the FAO, through its own regional commissions, in the process of formulating conservation measures, thereby making them direct contributors to the resolution of conflict.

As a consequence of extended coastal-state jurisdiction and increasing bilateral agreements between local and nonlocal fishing countries, it is likely that a global organization will from time to time be called upon to deal with questions which transcend the competence of many regional commissions or small collections of states. Our attention has already been called to several of these questions by the Department of Fisheries of the FAO; one of them is particularly important for management in light of current trends and deserves repetition.

> The Committee on Fisheries might also be a suitable forum to discuss the problems posed by an increasing number of fleets which are multi-national, fly by flag of a country which has no relation to the nationality of the operator, may be financed by capital from another, have crews largely from yet another country, may land their catches in others and may be based for lengthy periods elsewhere. Such a complexity of arrangements makes it difficult for the country of the operator to obtain adequate information about fishing activities, let alone exercise any control over them. The flag country of the vessel may not be interested in the stocks of fish exploited in diverse far-off areas. Also, as regional management measures become more effective, and restrictive, there will be a temptation for some operators to transfer their activities to a country which is not a party to the regional agreement.[27]

Admittedly, any attempt to expand COFI's role to include involvement in the activities outlined carries certain costs. It will require additional resources, primarily money and staff, to be allocated to the FAO Department of Fisheries, and it may increase conflict between member governments having different capabilities and interests. Specifically, countries with distant-water fishing capabilities may be unwilling to support budgetary increases for these activities. In any case, as a form of insurance, developing countries may wish to consider diverting a portion of revenues gained from joint ventures and licensing arrangements to supporting work *by the FAO* on stock assessment, fishery

---

[27] Food and Agriculture Organization, Committee on Fisheries, *Role of the FAO*, p. 8.

18

economics, and the implications of different regulatory techniques in areas of the ocean falling under their jurisdiction.

It is possible to minimize such conflict by avoiding a fight over statutory changes in COFI's terms of reference and by maintaining a neutral stance in the organization's work in stock assessment. At the same time it should be pointed out that there can be no guarantee of avoiding conflict which will adversely affect the organization's current work in stock assessment and technical assistance, even if members were to agree that COFI's role should not be expanded, albeit informally. This is so because expanding jurisdiction on the part of coastal states without the requisite expertise in management will increase their demands for assistance from the FAO. Moreover, interviews with delegates make it clear that many developing countries place a high priority on the FAO as a medium compensating for their lack of capability; this is reinforced by the fact that the FAO, through its technical assistance programs, has been responsible for training many of the people who now head fisheries administrations in developing countries. Thus, there is a legacy of rapport here extending to regional commissions sponsored by the FAO as an alternative to treaty-based commissions involving nonlocal fishing countries with great capabilities. This, for example, seems to be the case in the Indian Ocean.

GLOBAL MANAGEMENT
OF HIGHLY MIGRATORY SPECIES

Tuna

On the basis of work done by the FAO Expert Panel for the Facilitation of Tuna Research, it is clear that this is one case in which the merging of organizations will increase the effectiveness of management.[28] The mobility of the resource combined with the

[28] See the excellent report by John L. Kask, *Tuna: A World Resource,* Law of the Sea Institute, Occasional Paper no. 2 (Kingston: University of Rhode Island, 1969). See also Food and Agriculture Organization, Committee on Fisheries, *Some Problems of Management,* pp. 9–11, and *Other Urgent Problems of Rational Utilization of Fishery Resources: Atlantic Tuna* (Doc. no. COFI/68/6), 15 February 1968; Dale Broderick, "Law of the Sea Negotiations and the Tuna Fishery," in Alexander, ed., *The Law of the Sea: A New Geneva Conference,* pp. 213–216; J. Joseph, "The Scientific Management of the World Stocks of Tunas, Billfishes and Related Species" (Paper presented at the FAO Technical Conference, Vancouver, February 13–23, 1973); and Saila and Norton, "Alternative Arrangements."

mobility of fleets operating in the Atlantic, Pacific, and Indian oceans produce a need for a truly global approach in both stock assessment and the formulation of management measures. Extensions of coastal-state jurisdiction will not change this need in any significant way, since no single jurisdiction will cover a sufficiently large portion of the resource.

Alternative courses of action have already been defined by the FAO, and, though members of COFI have shown a marked reluctance to move toward centralization, events in the fisheries are likely to heighten the need for such a decision in the near future. There are three possible choices:

a) to ensure closer working arrangements between the different bodies;
b) to combine them in some way into a single body, possibly by extending the area of competence of one body;
c) to set up *ab initio* a new worldwide body.[29]

As a means of avoiding the lengthy negotiations involved in creating a new body and the inadequacies of closer working arrangements in "representing the interests of those not fishing in the area of one body, but indirectly affected by its actions,"[30] the FAO would appear to favor the second alternative. But since members of COFI are not yet ready to take this step, it may well come about in stages, particularly after the first alternative is tried and found wanting. This is likely to happen when the need for more comprehensive information on the stock is combined with regulatory problems, such as the timing of seasons, particularly between the Pacific and Atlantic oceans. Certainly, there is a need to evaluate possible arrangements under which the research will be done, if and when the Inter-American Tropical Tuna Commission (IATTC) and the Atlantic Commission (ICCAT) are merged, but these do not present insurmountable problems. After the necessary global organizational arrangements have been made, the difficult problems will continue to be those of arriving at limitations on effort and agreeing on the distribution of income.

Whales

The situation concerning whales is similar to that of tuna only in the sense that extended coastal-state jurisdiction will not make much difference in the existing regulatory arrangements for the

---

[29] Food and Agriculture Organization, Committee on Fisheries, *Some Problems of Management*, p. 10.
[30] *Ibid.*, p. 11.

Antarctic. A global organization, the International Whaling Commission (IWC), has been in existence for a long time. However, during the 1950s and early 1960s, in an attempt by the major whaling countries to retrieve capital investment in whaling fleets, the quotas agreed upon tended consistently to be much too high for the stocks to bear.[31] In fact, in the words of one experienced observer: "the result was not a conservation of Antarctic whales, but an orderly plunder of them, rather than a disorderly plunder."[32]

The situation has changed considerably since 1965, when agreements were arrived at in the IWC to protect the blue whale. At the same time, it has not yet been possible to arrive at agreement on adequate conservation measures covering the fin whale and some local stocks of sperm whales. The questions raised here for a global organization like the FAO relate once again to the scientific advisory work in stock assessment and to the formulation of conservation measures, rather than to the method of implementing these measures through decentralized negotiations on national quotas.

The fact is that the IWC has only a part-time secretary and no full-time staff. While there is a scientific advisory body, the work was done largely by scientists representing their national governments and, consciously or unconsciously, the results of scientific work done tended to support the positions maintained by the respective governments. Consequently, it was impossible to arrive at precise estimates of sustainable yields. The results were given in ranges, and the method of arriving at agreement, particularly the need for universality, usually resulted in agreements on quotas in the upper halves of the ranges given. The only possible way out of this impasse lay in a late decision in the IWC to seek specialist assessments in population dynamics from experts selected from the FAO and from countries not involved in whaling.

There is a valuable lesson contained in that event. It is that the work in stock assessment on which regulation is based must be of the very highest quality, and it must at all costs preserve its neutrality in the face of intense competition and conflict over the distribution of wealth as defined by national quotas. If not, the

---

[31] *Ibid.*, pp. 3–9. See also the comprehensive statement by D. G. Chapman, "Management of International Whaling and North Pacific Fur Seals: Implications for Fisheries Management" (Paper presented at the FAO Technical Conference, Vancouver, February 13–23, 1973).

[32] Remarks made by Dr. Sidney Holt, formerly of FAO and then Secretary of the Intergovernmental Oceanographic Commission, in Alexander, ed., *The UN and Ocean Management*, pp. 68–69.

decentralized system of arriving at decisions will always yield compromises on catch levels too high for the stocks to bear.

Even though the performance of the IWC is currently better than its performance in the period 1945–64, there remains the scientific question for all exploited stocks of whales: What is the level of the sustainable yield? There are still large differences in the estimates of scientists of different countries, but as substantial reductions in whale catches are achieved and as information increases, disparities between these different estimates will tend to decrease. What possibilities are available for overcoming the deficiencies of IWC relative to stock assessment?

There appear to be three alternatives—to merge the IWC with the FAO, to make the IWC an FAO-sponsored agency, or to make no formal administrative changes between the FAO and IWC but significantly increase the priority of stock assessment on whales within the FAO and disseminate the results of such research on a continuous basis to all members of the IWC and likely new entrants to the fishery. The choice of an alternative should be dictated by some specified value or values which the players wish to optimize. The ones already recommended are providing for the highest quality research and preserving the neutrality of the body that does it. Consequently, the third alternative appears to be most appealing, because it would achieve this without raising the inevitable jurisdictional fight implied by the first two. The costs of choosing this alternative are obviously either an expansion of budgetary resources or a reallocation of priorities under existing constraints.

CONCLUSIONS

The result of maintaining the criterion of feasibility is that only incremental changes have been considered. This paper has deliberately avoided the design and evaluation of alternatives which, for instance, assume the investment of exclusive rights in a single global organization, because there is virtually no possibility of getting such an alternative accepted in the current round of negotiations. In fact, all available evidence on the way major qualitative changes usually emerge in the international system, specifically with respect to peacekeeping, international monetary arrangements, and conservation of resources, suggests that major changes are possible only in the face of impending or recently experienced "disaster." This is defined as a general breakdown of the system and a dramatic increase in conflicts with widespread significant losses for all players.

Therefore, the argument has been that the relationship between technological advance and demands for jurisdictional changes in fisheries is bringing about changed relationships both between local and nonlocal fishing states and between coastal states. In this context the functions which a global research organization like FAO/COFI can be expected to perform in the near future are the following:

(1) data collection and analysis on a global basis;
(2) greater involvement in the formulation of conservation measures than previously, with particular attention being paid to assessing the probable impact of alternative measures;
(3) seeking a greater degree of coordination in the work of regional commissions than currently exists;
(4) continuation of its traditional role in technical assistance relative to education and training but expanding the advisory scope to include evaluation of joint ventures;
(5) greater involvement in the search for common arrangements and solutions to coastal-state conflict than previously. This also implies the assumption of management responsibilities on the part of FAO-sponsored regional commissions.

While these incremental changes do imply a need for increasing budgetary allocations in the Department of Fisheries of the FAO, they also create a possibility for member states to deal with each issue without having to face a general, potentially destructive jurisdictional fight. The flexibility, and even ambiguity, which this approach suggests would allow optimum room for maneuvering by the leadership in both the Committee on Fisheries and the Secretariat, thereby enhancing opportunities for innovative definitions of problems and alternative solutions.